How To Make Money Online Fast

Step By Step Instructions On How To Work From Home Using Proven Internet Marketing Strategies

Argena Olivis

www.ArgenaOlivis.com

Bonus: Download Your Free Kindle Book Creation Course

Learn how to create and market your first kindle book online.

You can use this course to get started making money online.

Plus, when you subscribe you'll receive my best tips and tutorials for online business success.

Learn how I'm making money from the following methods: kindle publishing, affiliate marketing, email marketing, information products, blogging, and more.

For Access Visit:

www.ArgenaOlivis.com/FreeKindleCourse/

Table of Contents

Introduction

I want to thank you and congratulate you for downloading the book, *"Make Money Online Fast: Step By Step Instructions on How to Work from Home Using Proven Internet Marketing Strategies"*.

This book contains proven steps and strategies on how to make money online fast using internet marketing practices that are working today. Many strategies that are being taught these days may take a while to see results. This book is for the person who wants to make their first dollar online just to prove to themselves that it can be done.

In this book I'm going to go into the fastest ways to make money online, and how to do each strategy in depth to get you started on the right path.

Over the years, I've invested hundreds, if not thousands, of dollars on information products and have done hours and hours of research on how to make money online.

I myself once had hopes of making money online, and now that I am, I'm going to share with you what's working in today's online business world.

I'm also going to take you step by step into how to do each of these strategies and give you some of my best tips on how to be successful with each.

You're probably wondering where you should start and what you should do first to make your first dollar online.

It's hard being new to making money online. There are so many shiny objects and marketers trying to get you to buy their products.

Most of the products are quality-- some are not.

Your best bet is to choose one of the methods in this to start making money, then use that method to hit your income goal and move on to the next.

Some of these methods tie into each other. But, don't worry, I'm going to show you exactly what to do.

This is not "get rich quick" book, but a "make money fast" book. You may not get rich off these strategies, but you will make money if you take action.

Thanks again for downloading Make Money Online Fast,

I hope you enjoy it!

Chapter 1: Kindle Publishing

Wow, where do I begin? You should know that I started my online journey in 2012. I was in college and looking for a way to make some extra money online.

That's when I came across website creation. While researching how to create a website on YouTube, I was shocked to find that there were people making tons of money online.

That's when I started going from the mindset of "I want to make money online" to "I want to create an online business."

As the story goes, I started reading business books,

buying courses, and of course building websites.

Many of the websites I built failed and never made a profit. Then everything changed, I decided I didn't want to work a job, I wanted to be an entrepreneur full time.

So I started to really focus on making an income online. I purchased two courses that then changed my life.

I started taking massive action and now I'm here, making a decent income online and writing this book to you-- the person who also has dreams of making their first dollar online.

Believe me, this stuff really works. You just have to change your mindset and really do the work.

None of these strategies work, without work. You may find yourself up late and up early, or sacrificing your TV time to try to make this work.

Whatever you do, if you truly want to make it, you have to put in the time and you have to want it bad enough.

I found that Kindle Publishing is by far the fastest method of making money online. This is because Amazon is the number one website that people shop.

So if you know what you're doing, you can truly clean up on Amazon.

How to Create a Kindle Book

The "how to" of creating a Kindle book is pretty simple, optimizing it so that it can be found is the hard part.

Yes, Amazon has a lot of customers, but it also has a lot of authors. More and more people are publishing Kindle books every single day, and every day the marketplace is becoming more saturated.

It's one of those things where you better get in when you can.

Step 1: Decide what market or niche that you want to write your book in. You have options to write nonfiction books, fiction books, erotica, and children's books.

It should be a niche you're familiar with. If you do decide to write a book in a niche you're not familiar with, make sure to do the proper research in order to create a quality book.

It's important that the niche that you write your book in is profitable.

If you decide to write a nonfiction book, look up the keyword that you want to target in your niche in the Amazon Kindle store. If you see books on the first page for the keyword, and the books have ranks under 100,000 then it's a profitable niche.

To find out more information on how to do keyword research and find profitable niches visit:

http://www.argenaolivis.com/kindle-keyword-research/

Typically books with an Amazon sales rank lower than 100,000 are making $30+ a month.

Step 2: Create a title for your book. When writing a nonfiction book use the keywords from the niche you've chosen. Your title should have relevant keywords in it, so it can be found easily in the kindle store.

Step 3: Open up a writing document of your choice and type out your book. Open Office and Microsoft Word are the most popular.

Depending on how familiar you are with the subject, you can finish your book in a day. I typically try to write for 1 hour a day, so I can finish books in about 5-7 days.

If you're writing a children's book, you will have to hire an illustrator. You can find low priced illustrators by going to www.Fiverr.com or Odesk.com. Unless of course, you yourself are an illustrator.

Your book does not have to be long, but it does have to be quality if you truly want to make sales. Bad reviews can slow down or eliminate your sales.

Unless it's a children's book, your book should be 15 or more pages.

You can find a template online by Googling "Kindle publishing templates" if you want to use a template to guide your writing.

Your nonfiction book should include an introduction, 4-6 chapters, and a conclusion. You can also add an about the author section, a squeeze page to capture emails, and a preview of another book.

Step 4: Upload your book to KDP. Go to www.kdp.amazon.com if you haven't done so yet, open up a KDP account.

Add all the necessary information about your book into KDP. The whole process is pretty self-explanatory, so you'll be able to enter the necessary information.

Step 5: Design your cover using the Kindle Cover Creator. The Kindle Cover Creator is a free software by

Amazon that you can use to create your book covers. They give you free templates, it's really cool. If you're creative and design well, this tool will be very beneficial to you.

If not, I suggest going to www.fiverr.com and ordering your cover for only $5. Or depending on how much you're willing to invest, you can also find freelancers to design your cover on Upwork.com.

Then you're finished. The process gets easier as you continue to create more and more books.

If your book is not selling, consider this:

- the niche may be too competitive

- you're not using the correct keywords

- you have a lot of bad reviews

- your cover is not attractive enough

There are many factors that go into rather or not your book sells. Make sure you enroll your book in the KDP select program in order to have a free promotion for your book.

These free promotions are for 5 days every three months. When a lot of people download your book it will help your book rank for its keywords.

So now the thing to do is take action. Use this guide and start creating your Kindle book today. The sooner you get it up, the faster you make money online!

Discover more ways to promote your kindle book by taking my video course on how to create and market your first kindle book:

http://www.argenaolivis.com/freekindlecourse

Chapter 2: Affiliate Marketing

Affiliate marketing is the second easiest way to make money online.

Affiliate marketing is when you promote someone else's product and get a commission for recommending the sale if the prospect purchases the product you're promoting through your affiliate link.

The great thing about affiliate marketing is that you're able to promote products on various platforms: social media, blogs, email, etc.

How to Get Started With Affiliate Marketing

You first need to find a target market. What type of topic are you interested in talking about?

Next, you need to make sure whatever market you want to get into has a product to promote. You can do this by searching in Google for affiliate programs for your market.

The things to look out for before joining an affiliate program:

- how much you'll make per referral/sale

- how long does the tracking cookie stay on the prospects browser

- how much support and help does the company give

- how much success are other promoters having

with the product

Some affiliate programs offer a ton of support. Some even offer you email swipes and ads you can use to promote their product.

Bonuses

The best way to get people to buy products through your affiliate link is to offer bonuses if they buy through your link.

Ideas for bonuses:

- free consultation

- eBook

- course

- guide on how to use the product

- audio

There are many bonuses you can create for your prospective customers.

The bonus will entice them to buy through your link.

Ask them to you their receipt for proof that they purchased through your affiliate link.

Keep in mind that your bonus should be relevant to the product you're promoting. It should complement the product.

This is a win-win. Because the prospect may have purchased the product anyway; but now they get an incentive for purchasing through you.

Resources Page

A resources or products page is a page that you create on your website that lists products that you use and or recommend.

If you don't have a website, you can get step-by-step instructions on how to create one by going to http://www.argenaolivis.com/website

Once you know what the topic of your website is, you can create a resources page to recommend products that your visitors will find valuable and relevant.

Make sure this page is on the main navigation bar of your site, this page can easily become the page that makes you the most income.

Use your affiliate link when recommending these products.

To see an example of a resources page, visit: http://www.argenaolivis.com/resources/

More on how to create blogs and website creation in a later chapter.

Product Demonstrations

You can use product demonstrations in order to get affiliate sales. A product demo is when you show how the product you're recommending is used.

Demonstrate how the product can be used to benefit the prospect.

You can do product demonstrations by recording video. Make sure to use the correct keywords when placing the video on YouTube and other video sharing sites in order to get the most exposure for your demonstration.

Highlight the benefits and features of the product, tell the prospect how the product will make their life easier or better.

Product Reviews

Review the products you have used and are an affiliate for.

Make sure that you highlight the benefits of the product and what you liked and didn't like about it.

When you tell prospects what you didn't like about it, it makes the review more genuine and they'll respect you for that.

No product is perfect, so tell what the product lacked and how it has made your life better.

Tips for Success

Make sure to always provide value. Don't just try and shove a product down a potential buyer's throat, make sure that they've gotten some type of value from you first.

Take your time and create great bonuses that are relevant to the product you're promoting.

Always use the product you're promoting. If you can, get the owner of the product to send you a sample. But it's best when it's something you've purchased yourself because you needed it at the time.

Be yourself and do your best. Put your customers first and make sure to collect their contact information by getting them on your email list; so that way you can promote other relevant products they can use to them at a later time.

Chapter 3: Email Marketing

Email marketing is the third easiest way to make money, it would be the first but it takes a little time to build your list.

Creating an email list is a valuable asset for your business because no matter what platform you use if your account or website gets shut down, you'll have a list of your customers that you can easily get in contact with to let them know what's going on.

Keep in mind that you're going to be building a relationship with the people on your list by creating valuable content that is relevant to the topic of your choice.

Email marketing has many benefits:

- instant sales

- relationship builder

- drives traffic to your website or products

- passivity

You are able to create auto-responders, which are pre-made messages that can go out to your list without you having to be there.

Or you can send out a broadcast to your list in real time about your product or an affiliate product that you're promoting and make instant sales.

The possibilities are endless. But first, you have to build your list the right way.

Creating an Opt-In Offer

An opt-in offer is something that you offer prospects for free in exchange for their name and email.

This should be something of value, and it should be something that is relevant to your niche.

Make your offer something that your prospect can download instantly, this means it should be a digital product. Here are some examples:

- 7 day email course/ boot camp

- video course

- eBook

- printables

- guide

- free report

- audio/ recorded conference call

You get the idea, make it something that can easily be downloaded and consumed.

Also, you have to make sure it's something that your target market will actually want.

You can test different opt-in offers to see what works best.

You have two options: your prospect can have the offer given to them as soon as they enter their name and or email, or after they confirm their subscription on the thank you page.

In order to collect names and emails, you're going to need an email service that will take care of hosting all your email addresses and messages.

I use a service called Aweber, learn more about it by going to http://www.argenaolivis.com/email-marketing-101/

Making Money from Your List

You can make money from your list by setting up autoresponder messages that provide your target market with valuable free content.

This can be content that is already on your blog, all you have to do is put a link back to the post and tell them what it's about.

You truly don't need a blog to make money with email marketing, you can just have a landing page/squeeze page where you collect the prospects name and email and provide them with content in through email.

Then after you've provided them with tons of value, you can send them an offer to something that is paid. This can be an affiliate product or your own product. Make sure the product is relevant and is can be used by your target market.

Start off with lower-priced items in the $3-$7 range and work your way up.

The Thank You Page

If you decide to go with a high-quality email service such as Aweber, you can create a thank you page for when a prospect confirms their subscription to your email newsletter.

On the thank you page you can tell the prospect what to expect. Then to warm them up to selling, you can offer them a sale on a product, or an affiliate product.

Squeeze Page

Have a squeeze page/landing page where you can send prospects to learn more about your opt-in offer.

Make sure this page really sales the opt-in offer and gives them a reason to want to enter their name and email. There is so much email spam these days that many people don't feel comfortable giving out their email addresses.

This should be the most frequently promoted page on your site.

You don't need a website to make money with this method, all you need is to drive traffic to your squeeze page in order to collect contact information.

Drive Traffic to Your Opt-In Offer

You want to make sure to promote your offer as much as you can to get your prospect's email addresses.

Here are some ways to get email subscribers:

- YouTube video description

- Social Media: Facebook, Twitter, Google +, Pinterest

- Guest Blogging

- Paid Ads

- Slideshare

- Forums

Those are just a few ways, but you can you can definitely get creative in getting more people on your list.

Chapter 4: Information Products

Information products are a pretty fast way to make money online. It's even easier if you already have an audience to promote it to. But there are ways around this.

An information product is a product that you create that contains valuable information. This can be in the form of a video course, eBook, or even audio files.

If someone can buy it online and it doesn't require shipping physical products, or you having to be there, it's an information product.

If you don't have an audience, your best bet is to go with

channels that allow you to create your product and market it to their already existing audience.

My favorite is Udemy. Udemy.com is a site that offers online courses. These courses are taught by instructors, like you and me. The catch is they keep a portion of your royalties as a courtesy of your exposure to their large audience.

Udemy is makes uploading your course very organized and convenient; and if you're teaching about something that people want to learn about, you can quickly make money online using their platform.

Or you can create your own information product. If your product is quality and it serves a need, then it will sell.

Creating Your Product

There are many types of information products you can create. The most popular ones are eBooks and video courses.

EBook creation is similar to kindle book creation, but instead of submitting your word document to KDP select, you can export it as a secure pdf.

Now all you need is a website and a PayPal button, or any system that where you can collect payment and send the product over to the buyer right after they purchase your product.

Video courses can be a bit trickier. If you have a WordPress website, you can use the free plugin called Namaste to create your video course. But you'll still need a payment gateway, you can use s2Member which is also free.

If you're just recording yourself, you can use any high-quality video camera. But, if you want to record your screen you can use Screen-Cast-O-Matic or Jing. They are both quality and free options.

Edit and upload each video to your WordPress site and organize the videos accordingly. You can add extra materials to support all learning types; like pdfs or audios to go along with each video lesson.

As long as your course is organized, and you have the

payment and delivery set up, and it's a valuable and quality product, you're good to go.

Marketing Your Information Product

You can market your product to your email list. Or, if you don't have one yet you can become friends with people that are more successful than you in your niche, and if they like your product they can promote it to their email list.

You can create an affiliate program for your product. Put your product on places like Clickbank.com and have other people sell your product as an affiliate.

Run ad campaigns and do a big product launch for your

product to really get it out there.

You can truly make money online fast if you use this method, and if the product is quality and relevant people will only have great things to say about it.

Chapter 5: Blogging

The reason I put blogging as the last chapter is because it's truly one of the slowest ways to make money.

This is because there's so many blogs out there. Unless you have tons of time on your hands to promote your blog, or you connect with people that are already successful in your niche to help promote your blog, you won't make money fast.

This is why I suggest you create a community first. Once you have a community that's used to hearing from you and trust you, it'll be easy to sell to them.

There are a few tips that will help you with your website

or blog creation.

Tip #1: Use SEO (Search Engine Optimization) in order to get traffic to your website. SEO is when you use keywords people are searching for in the search engines to get found through the search engines.

If you create a WordPress website, you can download the plugin called SEO Yoast, it helps you stay on track with SEO for each page and post.

Tip #2: Create a niche site. Make a site that has one specific topic. By doing this, you'll have a target community to sell to when you start creating products.

Tip #3: Look for ways to drive traffic to your blog. Don't just create a blog post, make sure you're driving traffic to your site by creating videos and building a community using social media and email marketing. Another popular way is to create a podcast.

If you haven't yet created your website, no worries. You can visit www.argenaolivis.com/website for my step-by-step tutorial.

Make sure to have a resources page created right away. Find affiliate programs you can promote on your blog and in your blog posts.

Use the affiliate marketing strategies in chapter 2 in order to create content that will be more geared toward your prospect buying.

A large learning curve is involved in blogging, because you have to be motivated to create content, find out how to get traffic to it, find out how to monetize it; it can be very difficult if you're new to the arena.

There are so many shiny objects out there that can lead you astray from your focus, which is to make money online.

I think a blog is a great strategy to make money online, but I also believe that it's a long-term strategy unless you have some type of edge over the competition like your network or you have lots of money to promote it.

You also have to be unique. There are tons of blogs, so you have to make yours unique in some way.

All in all, creating a blog is advised, but it's not the fastest way to make money. But if you're trying to create a true business a blog is necessary.

Chapter 6: Your Plan Comes To Life

Every day you wait, you are missing out on opportunities to start making an income online.

It's time to take action. Use these strategies and methods to start making money online fast!

It's best if you start off with one strategy and move on to the next, but as you know, some of these methods will overlap.

Depending on how much time you have, how bad you want it, and how much you're willing to sacrifice, you can truly make money online fast!

Notice that the title of the book is not make money online easy, but fast.

I recommend starting off with a strategy that is proven and simple like Kindle publishing. It's hot right now, and people are waiting to hear what you have to say.

I've provided the information on how you can do it, now all you have to do is go out there and put it into action.

I don't know what your goals are, I don't know why you want to make money online. But I know you didn't read this entire book because you were bored, you picked this because you want something better.

You have what you need to get started, so let's get to it!

Conclusion

Thank you again for reading *Make Money Online Fast*!

I hope this book was able to help you to make money online fast.

The next step is to choose a strategy and get work.

Finally, if you enjoyed this book, then I'd like to ask you for a favor, would you be kind enough to leave a review for this book on Amazon? It'd be greatly appreciated!

By leaving a review, you'll be helping others to find the book. It will also give me feedback on what I can improve on or what I did well.

Thank you and good luck!

Preview of 'Email Marketing Machine'

Chapter 1: Establishing Your Target Market

How well do you know your customer? Do you know what they like to do? What their interests are? How you can help them? If not, that's okay we're going to learn all about that.

But first, you need to establish a niche if you haven't already. A niche is a specific topic that you want to focus on. You may already have a website, service, or product that already focuses on a specific topic.

There are some guidelines you need to follow when choosing your niche: profitability, knowledge, likeability, and size.

Profitability

Before you choose a niche, you want to ensure it's profitable. You can find this out by visiting Google.com and typing in your topic and seeing how other people are making money with this niche.

Visit a few of the top websites. If you choose this niche, these will be your competitors. Competition is a good thing, this means there's money to be made.

Don't worry too much about the size of their audience. The one thing that you can do differently is be yourself. Your competitor can never be you, you're original so make sure to use that as an advantage. You shouldn't dwell on what you cannot change.

Also, make sure you have a mindset of abundance. Believe that there's enough to go around for everyone. If you're coming from a place where you're adding value and serving your audience, there's plenty of room for you and your business.

You have to have the right mindset to succeed in business. So work on your self-growth and confidence first if you've been at this for a while and still haven't taken action.

When you visit your competitor's website, look to see how they're making money. Do they offer coaching? Do they have a brick in mortar? Services? Their own store or products and courses? Affiliate marketing?

This most likely will be how you will be making money too, so get some ideas and jot them down.

If the site you visit looks like they are making money with just advertising, you may want to stay away from that. Only because you don't want to put all your eggs in one basket.

If they have private ads from different companies, you may be onto something. But it's still too risky.

Do they have products or services in this niche? If they do, there's most likely people making money from it. This means it's profitable.

If you think about going into a niche that doesn't already have products or services, this will not be a smart move.

Internet marketing has been around for years, and if no one has created a product for your niche, then it's most likely not profitable because it doesn't have a big enough audience.

You ultimately want to make a profit, and you can't do that with a non-profitable niche.

Other techniques you can use is to see if your niche has products on big sites like Clickbank or Amazon.com.

Use Amazon search to your advantage by seeing if there are at books selling on the topic you're thinking about getting into.

Do this by typing in a keyword and seeing how profitable the book is. You can tell how profitable a book is by the rank. If it's below 100,000 in the paid kindle store, this means it's making some money.

Knowledge

How much knowledge and experience do you have in the niche? You're going to need it.

You can always study a particular niche, but that's going to take a lot of time and be difficult for you.

But if you have the money, you can always outsource content using services such as Odesk, Elance, and Fiverr.

If you truly want to learn more about the niche, consider doing a "journey". This is where you take people through your journey of that niche.

For example My site Argena Olivis is currently about my journey to online business success. I'm taking people on a journey and showing them how I'm creating multiple streams of income online.

You can do this with a niche to, but you truly have to be committed to learning a lot and growing over time so your audience can see progress.

You may be thinking that you can't find a niche because you're not necessarily good or passionate about anything in particular. Well, I think there has to be something you like a lot.

Think about how you spend your free time. Do you have any hobbies such as scrapbooking or fixing cars?

There's something you're good at. If you're truly struggling to find a niche, make sure to ask the people closest to you what they think you're good at and then try to find a profitable niche from there.

If you have a lot of money, and no time, consider outsourcing your content. This may be expensive, but it's totally worth it if you want to be in that niche.

You can do this by going to places like Fiver.com, Odesk.com, and Elance.com.

Likeability

You have to like the niche you choose. If you don't like it, you're not going to stick with it and it's not fair to your audience.

You don't have to be passionate about it, but you should, at least, find it interesting.

Its dangerous getting into a niche you don't believe in or that you don't truly like. It will show through your emails and your content that you don't enjoy it.

If you don't truly like it, stay away from it. It's not worth the money if your stomach turns every time you have to create content.

Like I said, you don't have to be passionate, but you should come from a place of wanting to help others.

Size

Make sure you choose a niche that is not too small or too broad.

Small niches can be great because you have a very specific target market. But you have to look at it from a profitability standpoint too. Don't niche down so far that you're only talking to 20 people.

Don't have your niche so big that you're targeting everybody. This is a mistake.

You can't please everyone so don't even try.

This will put a hindrance on building relationships, you can't build relationships through email if you're targeting every type of person.

Being able to stand out from the crowd also comes into play. You want to make sure you stand out and can differentiate yourself from the millions of business owners trying to make money online.

Example: You shouldn't create a market on general

weight loss for everyone. Niche down and create a site for weight loss for women. Niche down even further and create a site for weight loss for women in college.

I wouldn't niche down any further than that, but this would be a good target market. Do you get my drift? You want to know who your target market is so you can actually find them and help them out.

This comes back to knowledge and experience, what do you know? How can you being who you are, and where you are, be an advantage? Use that info to create your target market if it fits the guidelines.

If you get this part right and find a great target market, you'll make more money in the long run because you'll be able to connect with your audience better through your content and emails.

The Take Away

Please **do not skip this step** if you don't already have a target market! Without having a specific target market, you won't know who to advertise to and who to create emails for.

Know your target market and what stage they're at in life. Are they a beginner or more advanced or anywhere in between?

Once you know who to market to, your life becomes easier and you're able to help other people solve their problems and make money doing it.

If you already have a target market that's great. If not, go through these steps and decide on one. You can always change it later, but for now, you want to get started.

I want you to get results from this book. So decide on your target, take action.

Check Out My Other Books

Below you'll find some of my other popular books that are popular on Amazon and Kindle as well.

You can also visit my author page on Amazon to see other work done by me.

Email Marketing Machine: Using Email To Build Relationships, Traffic, and Make Money Online

Affiliate Marketing: How To Make Money With Other People's Products

Information Products For Beginners: How To Create and Make Money With Information

Kindle Publishing Back End: Guide To Create A Real Business With Kindle Publishing

Amazon FBA: Reselling Strategies For More Income On FBA

Online Business Mindset: Personal Development and Confidence Building For Internet Marketers

Fulfillment By Amazon For Beginners: Step By Step

Instructions On How To Make an Income With FBA

Bonus: Download Your Free Kindle Book Creation Course

Learn how to create and market your first kindle book online.

You can use this course to get started making money online.

Plus, when you subscribe you'll receive my best tips and tutorials for online business success.

Learn how I'm making money from the following methods: kindle publishing, affiliate marketing, email marketing, information products, blogging, and more.

For Access Visit:

www.ArgenaOlivis.com/FreeKindleCourse/

www.ingramcontent.com/pod-product-compliance
Lightning Source LLC
Chambersburg PA
CBHW070934180526
45168CB00003B/1077